draw around and
HOW TO DRAW
DINOSAURS

Written & designed by Anton Poitier
Illustrated by Hui Yuan Chang

BARRON'S

Let's get started!

This book shows you how to draw animals by drawing around shapes. All the shapes you need are at the back of the book. There are steps to draw every animal. There are also lots of hints and tips for making your drawings different!

There are three boards at the back of the book. Press out the shapes, as you need them. They are labeled.

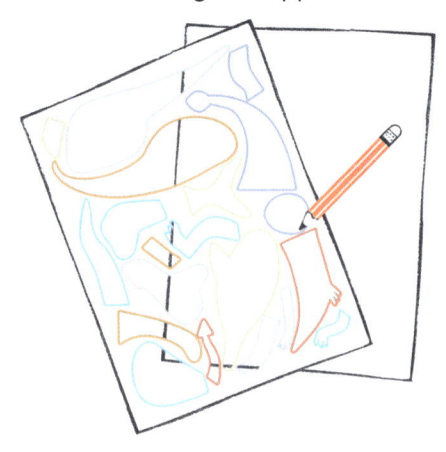

You can also use the press out sheet as a stencil. This is handy for the small parts, such as tails.

Start drawing!

❶ Begin by placing the first shape in the center of a piece of paper.

❷ Place the second shape where shown, and draw around it with a pencil.

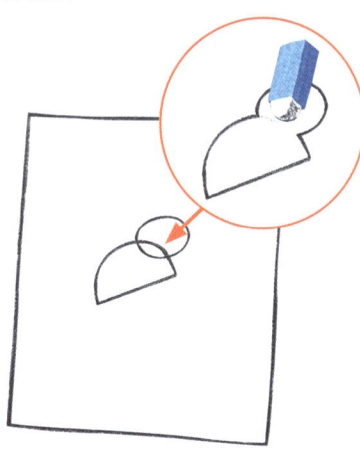

❸ Use an eraser to remove the pencil marks where they go over the shape underneath.

Tips to make your dino special

Add funny details.

Add details, such as eyes, teeth, and claws.

Use one main color for the body.

Make marks that suit your dinosaur, such as spots or stripes.

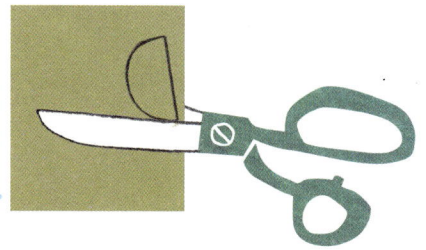

Instead of using white paper, you could use colored paper. Cut it out and paste it down to make your picture.

Coloring your pictures

Here are some handy tips. You can use colored pencils, felt-tip pens, crayons, or watercolor paint to complete your drawing. Water-soluble colored pencils work very well. The pictures in this book are colored in this way.

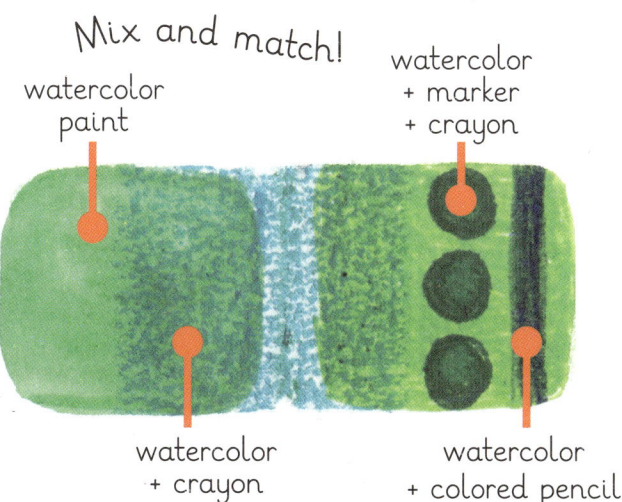

Blend the pencil colors with water.

Paint over the pencil with water.

Draw or paint different colors and shapes over the paint when it is dry.

Mix and match!

- watercolor paint
- watercolor + marker + crayon
- watercolor + crayon
- watercolor + colored pencil

Draw a scary T-Rex

The T-Rex had short arms with two claws on each arm. They were used as hooks to catch prey. Yikes!

Place his head like this on the page.

① Draw the head.

② Add the body.

③ Now, draw the front legs.

④ Add the back legs.

Find the T-Rex pieces at the back of the book. Set them out in front of you like this:

Draw a zigzag along the back.

Color your T-Rex with paint or colored pencils.

Add a ROAR, too!

The T-Rex was fierce!

Draw an open mouth!

Make your T-Rex look different!

Draw sharp teeth!

Notice the position of the body and head.

Turn the pieces over so that the T-Rex faces the other way.

A T-Rex in a museum!

Sketch a Stegosaurus

1 Draw the head.

The Stegosaurus was about 30 feet (9 m) long with a brain the size of a walnut!

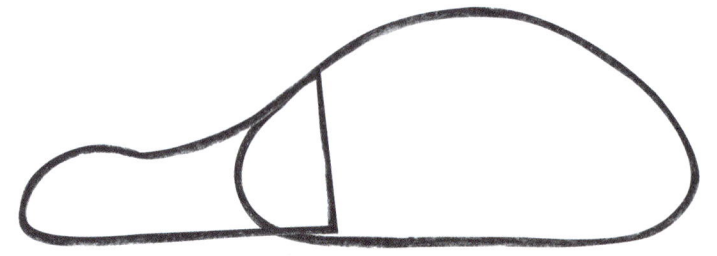

2 Add the body to the right of the head.

Keep the pieces flat along the bottom.

3 Now, draw the tail.

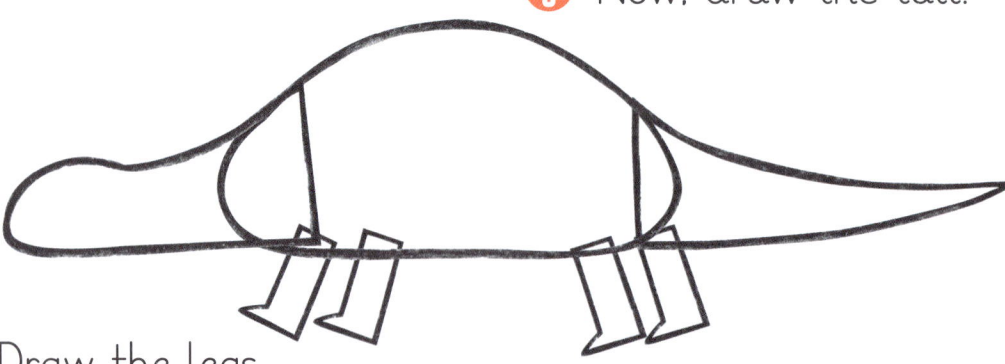

4 Draw the legs.

Find the Stegosaurus pieces at the back of the book. Set them out in front of you like this:

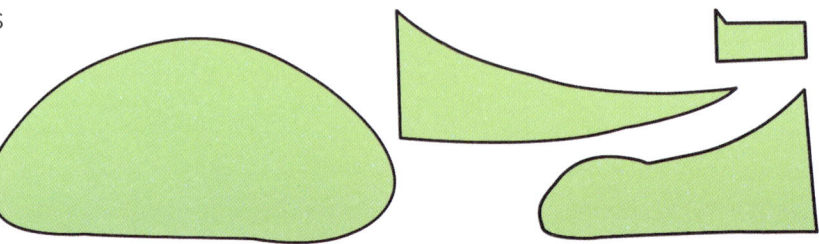

Draw spines along the back.

Invent a pattern for the body.

Color your Stegosaurus with paint or colored pencils.

Use your favorite colors!

Add diamond-shaped spines!

Give your Stegosaurus a smile!

Draw straight legs.

Make your Stegosaurus look different!

Draw an open mouth.

Turn the body up the other way.

7

Draw a Brontosaurus

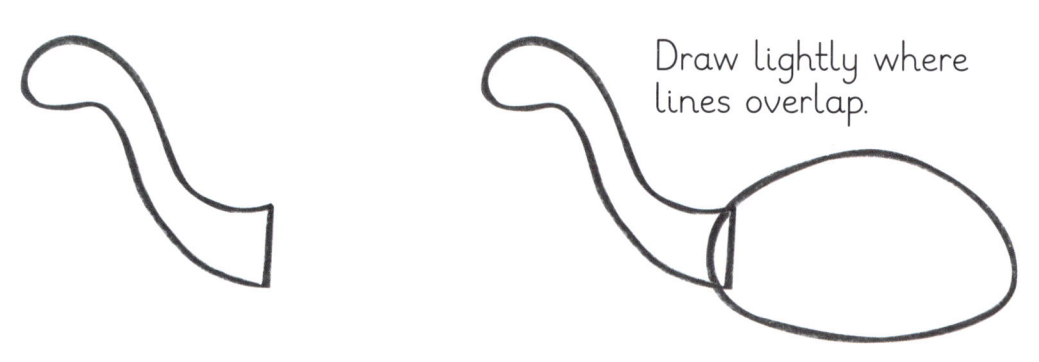

1. Draw the head and neck.

2. Now, draw the body. Draw lightly where lines overlap.

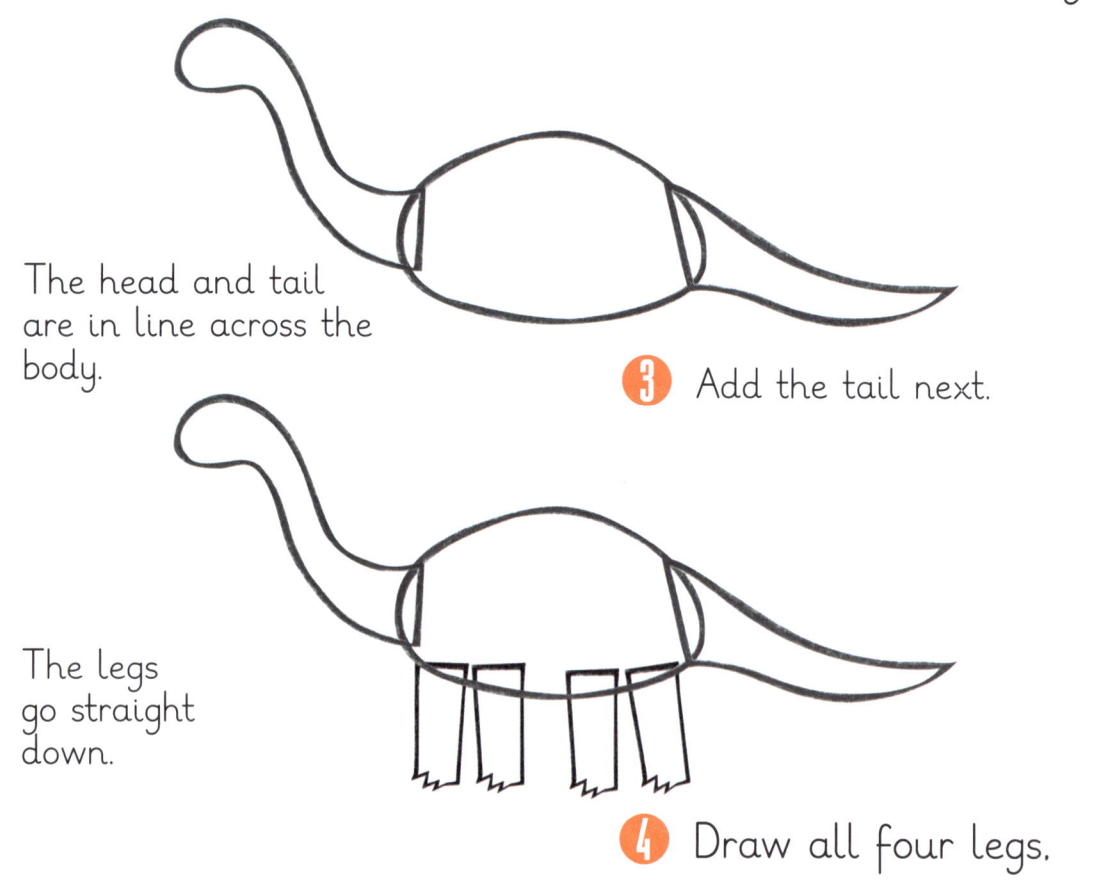

3. Add the tail next. The head and tail are in line across the body.

4. Draw all four legs. The legs go straight down.

Find the Brontosaurus pieces at the back of the book. Set them out in front of you like this:

Some people call the Brontosaurus by a different name: Apatasaurus.

The Brontosaurus was over 75 feet (23 m) long!

Give your Brontosaurus a happy face.

Make your Brontosaurus look different!

Turn the pieces over to make the dinosaur face the other way.

Draw your Brontosaurus in the sea!

Draw a spiky Triceratops

1 Draw the head.

Draw lightly where lines overlap.

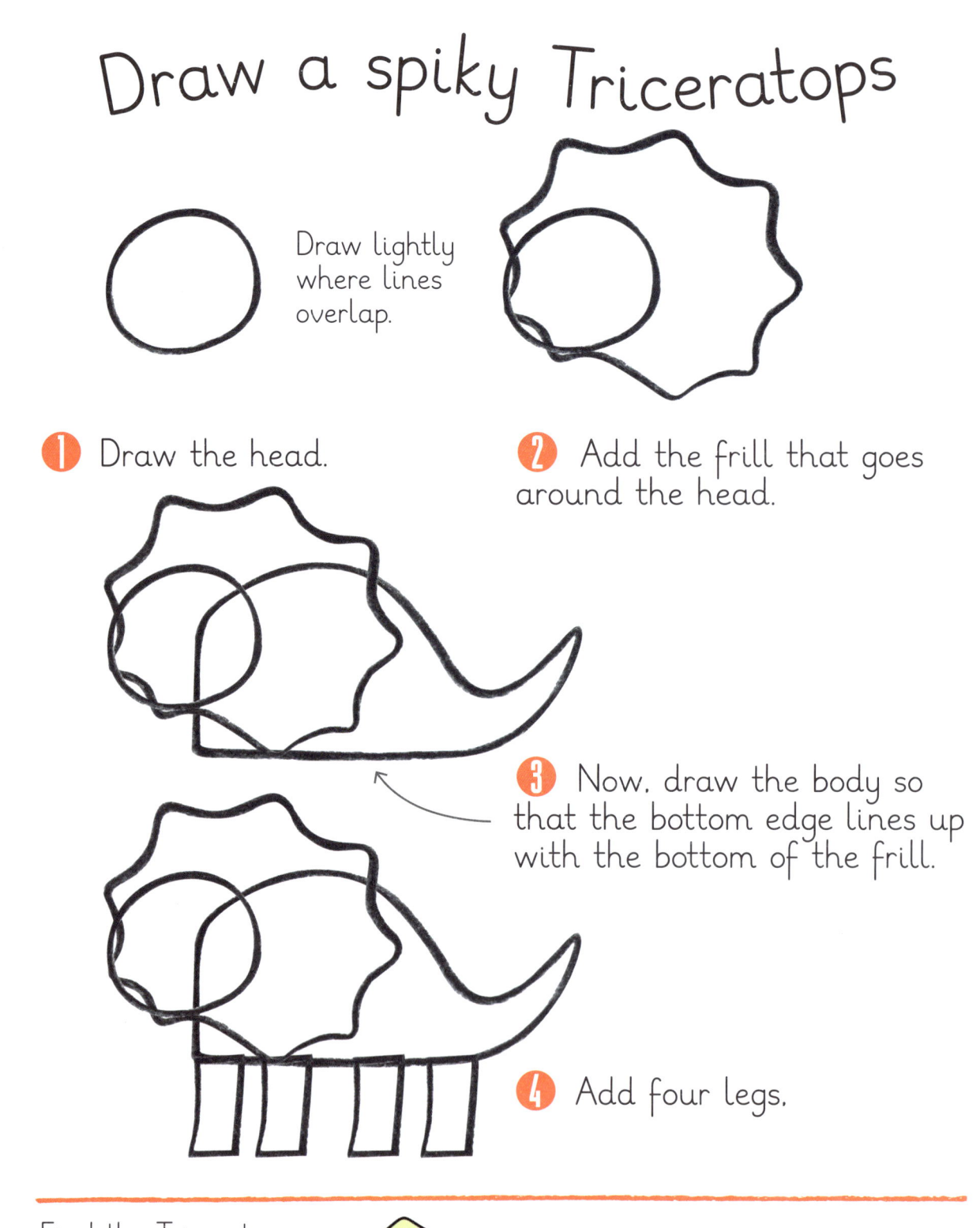

2 Add the frill that goes around the head.

3 Now, draw the body so that the bottom edge lines up with the bottom of the frill.

4 Add four legs.

Find the Triceratops pieces at the back of the book. Set them out in front of you like this:

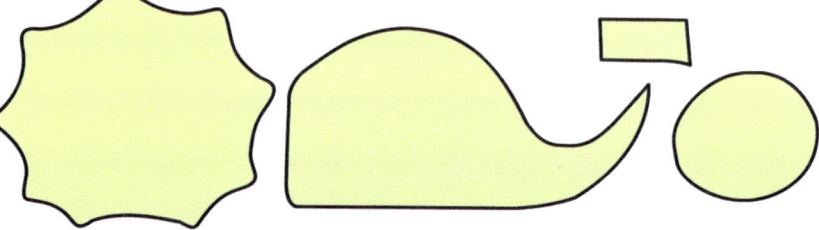

10

Draw an open mouth.

Triceratops means "three-horned face." This dinosaur was about 30 feet (9 m) long!

Add eyes, nostrils, and horns!

Your Triceratops can be any color you like!

Make your Triceratops look different!

Change the leg positions.

Turn the head the other way.

The head could also face forward like this one.

11

Draw an Ankylosaurus

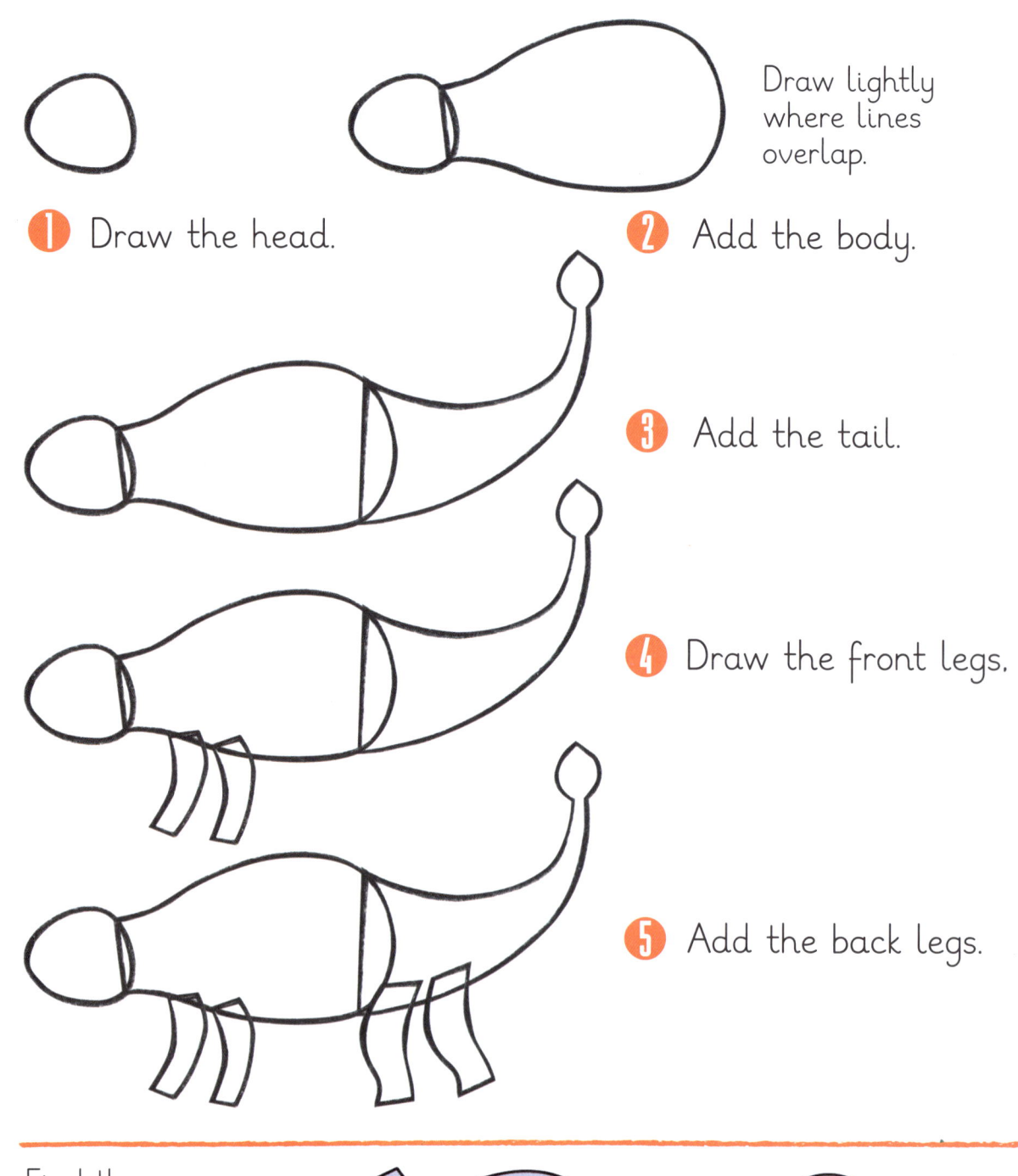

Draw lightly where lines overlap.

1. Draw the head.
2. Add the body.
3. Add the tail.
4. Draw the front legs.
5. Add the back legs.

Find the Ankylosaurus pieces at the back of the book. Set them out in front of you like this:

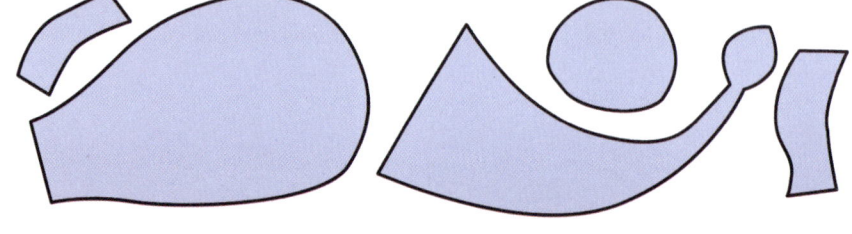

Make your Ankylosaurus look friendly by copying this mouth shape.

Add lots of spikes all over the body!

Add some flowers!

The Ankylosaurus used the club at the end of its tail to bash other dinosaurs!

Make your Ankylosaurus look different!

Draw the tail pointing down.

Draw a fierce face!

The Ankylosaurus was about 30 feet (9 m) long!

Tip the body forward.

Change the leg positions.

Draw a Diplodocus

Draw lightly where lines overlap.

1 Draw the head.

2 Add the body.

3 Now, draw the legs.

Find the Diplodocus pieces at the back of the book. Set them out in front of you like this:

14

The Diplodocus was about 115 feet (35 m) long—the length of 7 cars!

Take your Diplodocus for a walk!

Add a saddle and rider!

Draw a pattern on the back.

Add some flowers!

Make your Diplodocus look different!

Turn the body upside down like this.

Draw little trees to make your Diplodocus look huge!

Change the leg positions.

Draw a Velociraptor

Draw lightly where lines overlap.

1 Draw the head.

2 Next, add the body.

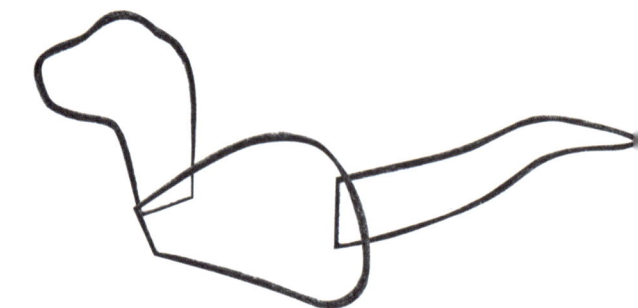

3 Draw the tail.

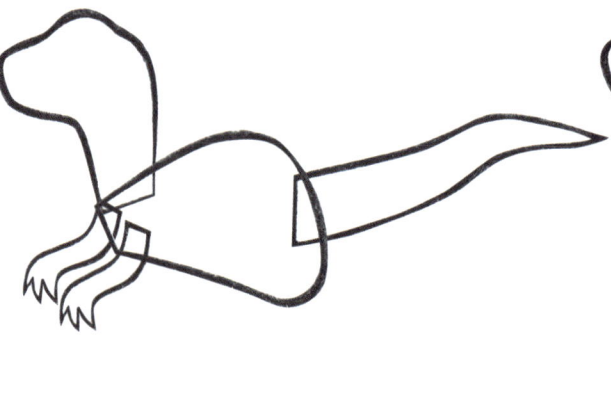

4 Add the front legs.

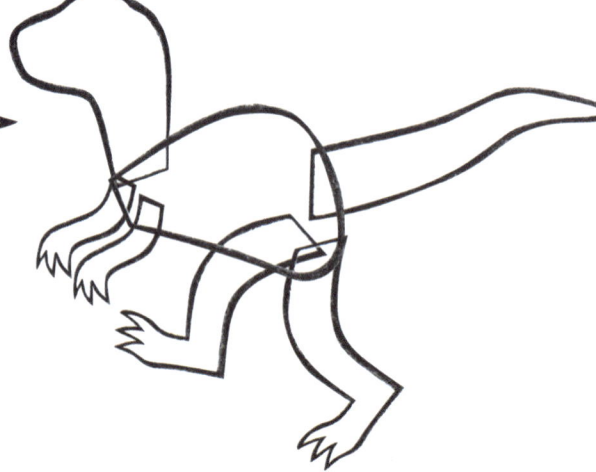

5 Draw the back legs.

Find the Velociraptor pieces at the back of the book. Set them out in front of you like this:

The Velociraptor was about the height of a Labrador Retriever and had sharp claws to kill its prey.

I have a bright idea!

Add sharp teeth to make me fierce!

Turn the head around.

Make your Velociraptor look different!

Draw open jaws.

You could draw spots or stripes. No one knows the true color of any dinosaur!

Draw a Corythosaurus

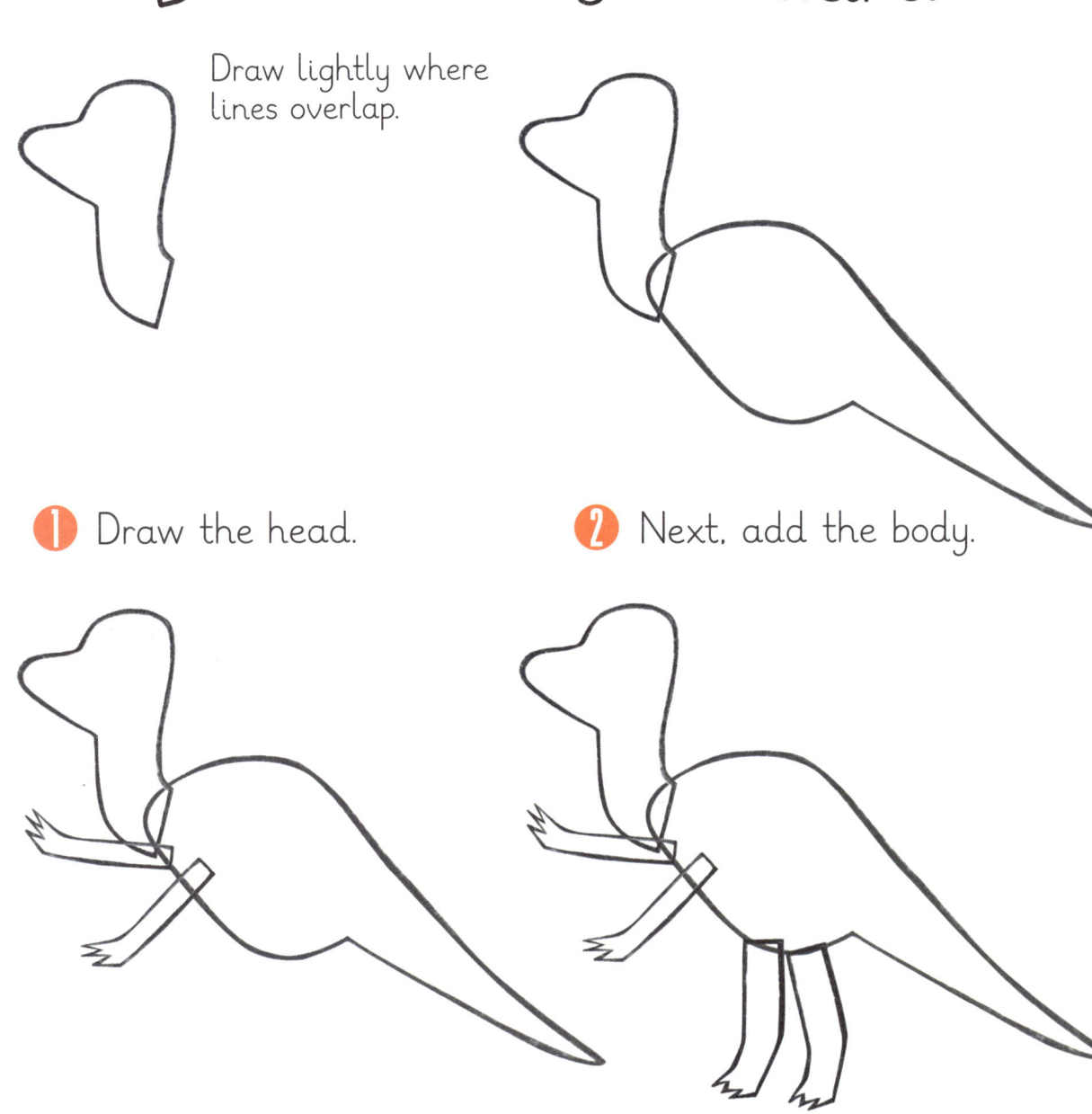

Draw lightly where lines overlap.

① Draw the head.

② Next, add the body.

③ Add the front legs.

④ Now, draw the back legs.

Find the Corythosaurus pieces at the back of the book. Set them out in front of you like this:

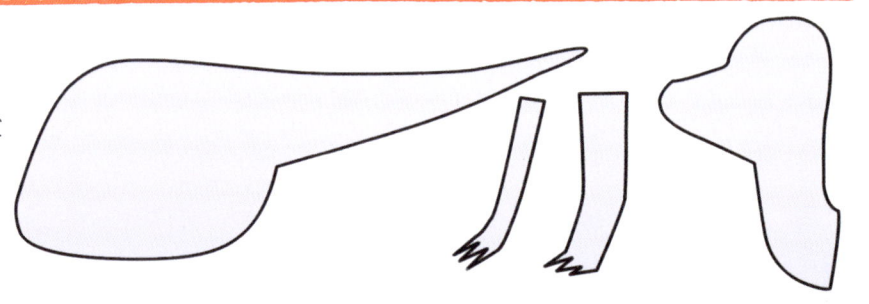

Corythosaurus means "helmet head" after the helmet-like crest on top of the head. People think this was used to make a loud horn noise.

Choose your favorite colors!

Draw a plant for your Corythosaurus to eat.

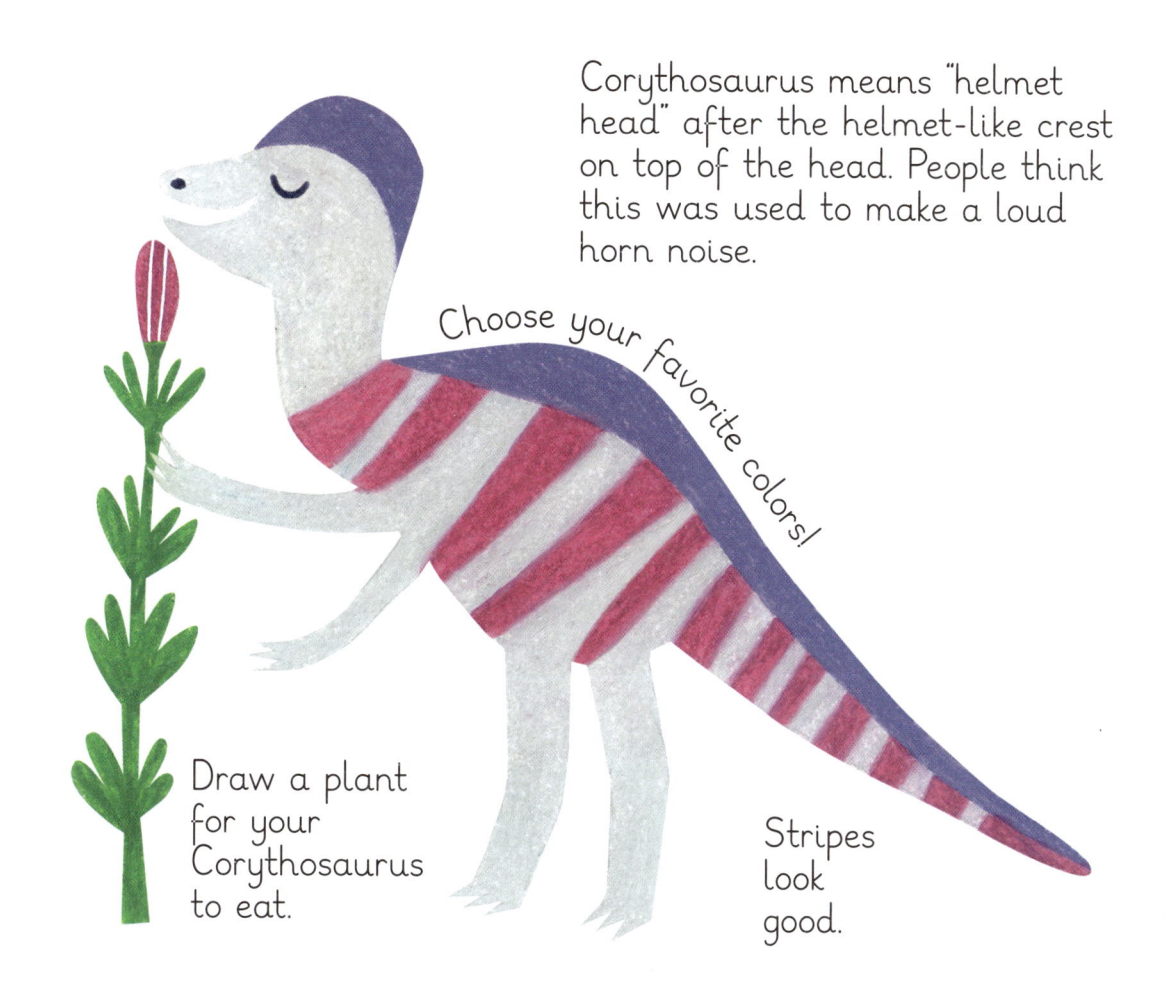

Stripes look good.

Make your Corythosaurus look different!

Draw stripes on the helmet and back.

Change the leg positions.

Turn the body upside down.

19

Draw an Ichthyosaurus

Draw lightly where lines overlap.

❶ Draw the head and the middle part of the body.

❷ Next, add the tail.

❸ Draw the fins.

Find the Ichthyosaurus pieces at the back of the book. Set them out in front of you like this:

20

Color your Ichthyosaurus so that the mouth is open.

Ichthyosaurus means "fish lizard."

Make your Ichthyosaurus look different!

Make an open mouth by moving the head a little when you draw around it.

Change the tail position.

Draw spots or stripes.

Add bubbles.

21

Draw a Plesiosaurus

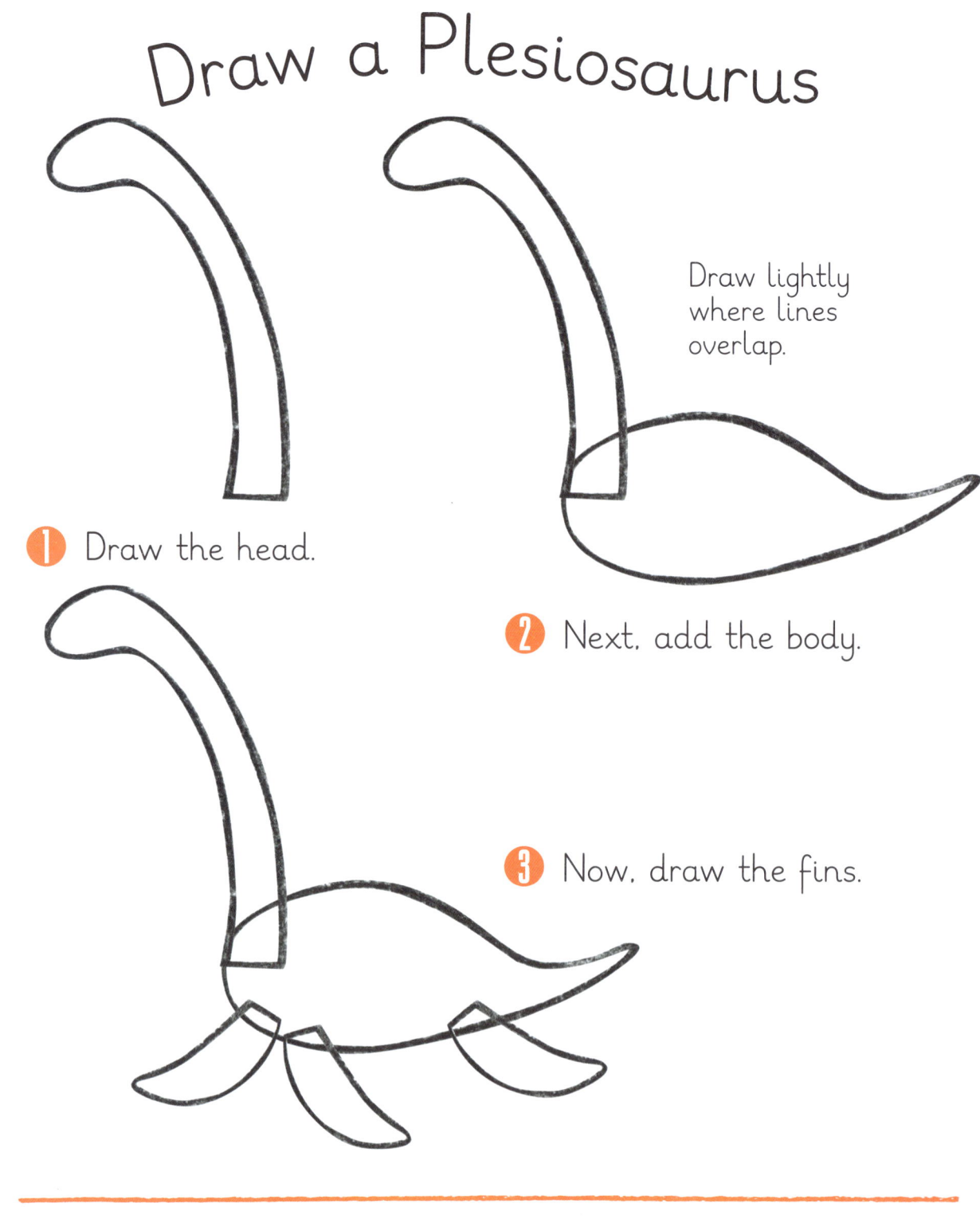

Draw lightly where lines overlap.

① Draw the head.

② Next, add the body.

③ Now, draw the fins.

Find the Plesiosaurus pieces at the back of the book. Set them out in front of you like this:

The Plesiosaurus lived in the sea. It had sharp teeth and grew to about 55 feet (17 m) long.

The Plesiosaurus lived until about 65 million years ago.

People who believe in the Loch Ness Monster think it is like a Plesiosaurus.

Draw a pattern on the back!

Make your Plesiosaurus look different!

Add a spaceship!

Add some water.

Draw a Pterosaur

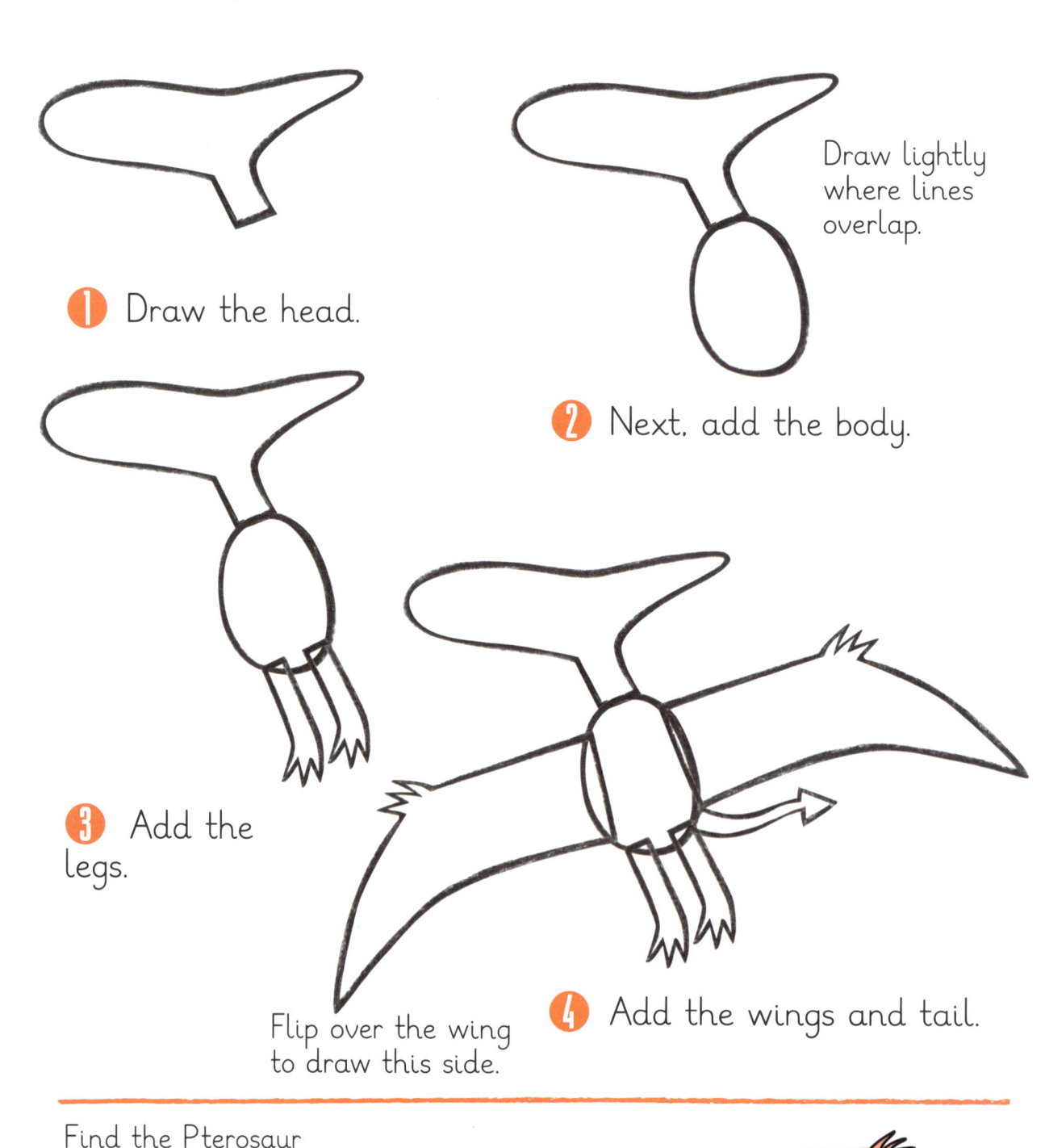

1. Draw the head.

2. Next, add the body.

   Draw lightly where lines overlap.

3. Add the legs.

4. Add the wings and tail.

   Flip over the wing to draw this side.

Find the Pterosaur pieces at the back of the book. Set them out in front of you like this:

Add sharp teeth.

Pterosaur means "winged lizard."

Color the wings so that you can see the bones.

Draw a fish in its jaws.

Make your Pterosaur look different!

Turn the wings around so that they flap downward.

Change the angle of the head.

Draw the legs straight out instead of downward.

Choose your favorite colors!

The biggest Pterosaur had a wingspan of up to 36 feet (11 m)!

25

Draw a Spinosaurus

1. Draw the head.

2. Next, add the body.

Draw lightly where lines overlap.

3. Add the tail.

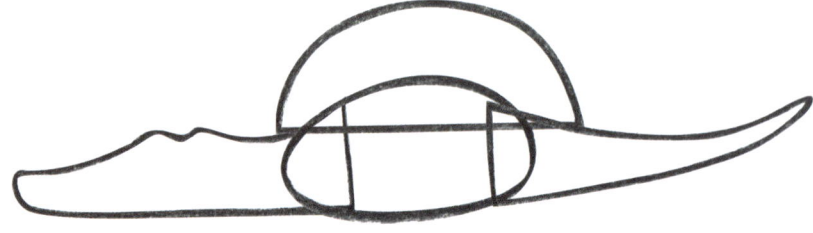

4. Now, draw the spine shape.

5. Draw the front and back legs.

Find the Spinosaurus pieces at the back of the book. Set them out in front of you like this:

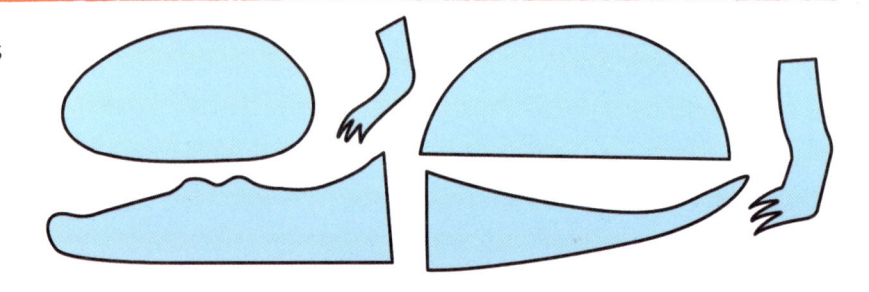

26

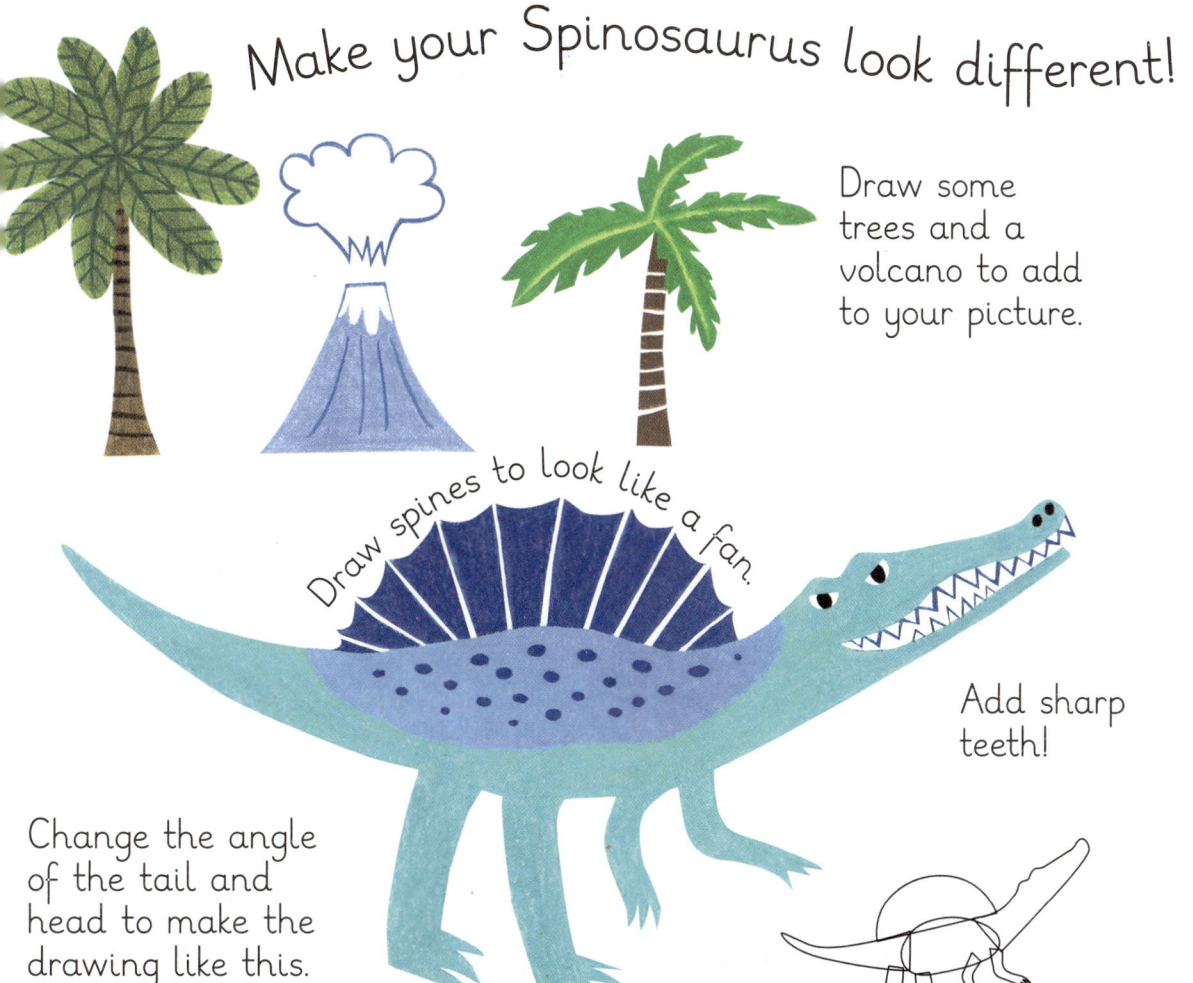

The Spinosaurus was larger than the T-Rex and may have been the biggest meat eating dinosaur ever!

Spinosaurus means "spine lizard."

Draw a zigzag shape to make the spines.

Add some water, too!

Make your Spinosaurus look different!

Draw some trees and a volcano to add to your picture.

Draw spines to look like a fan.

Add sharp teeth!

Change the angle of the tail and head to make the drawing like this.

27

Draw an Iguanodon

1 Draw the head.

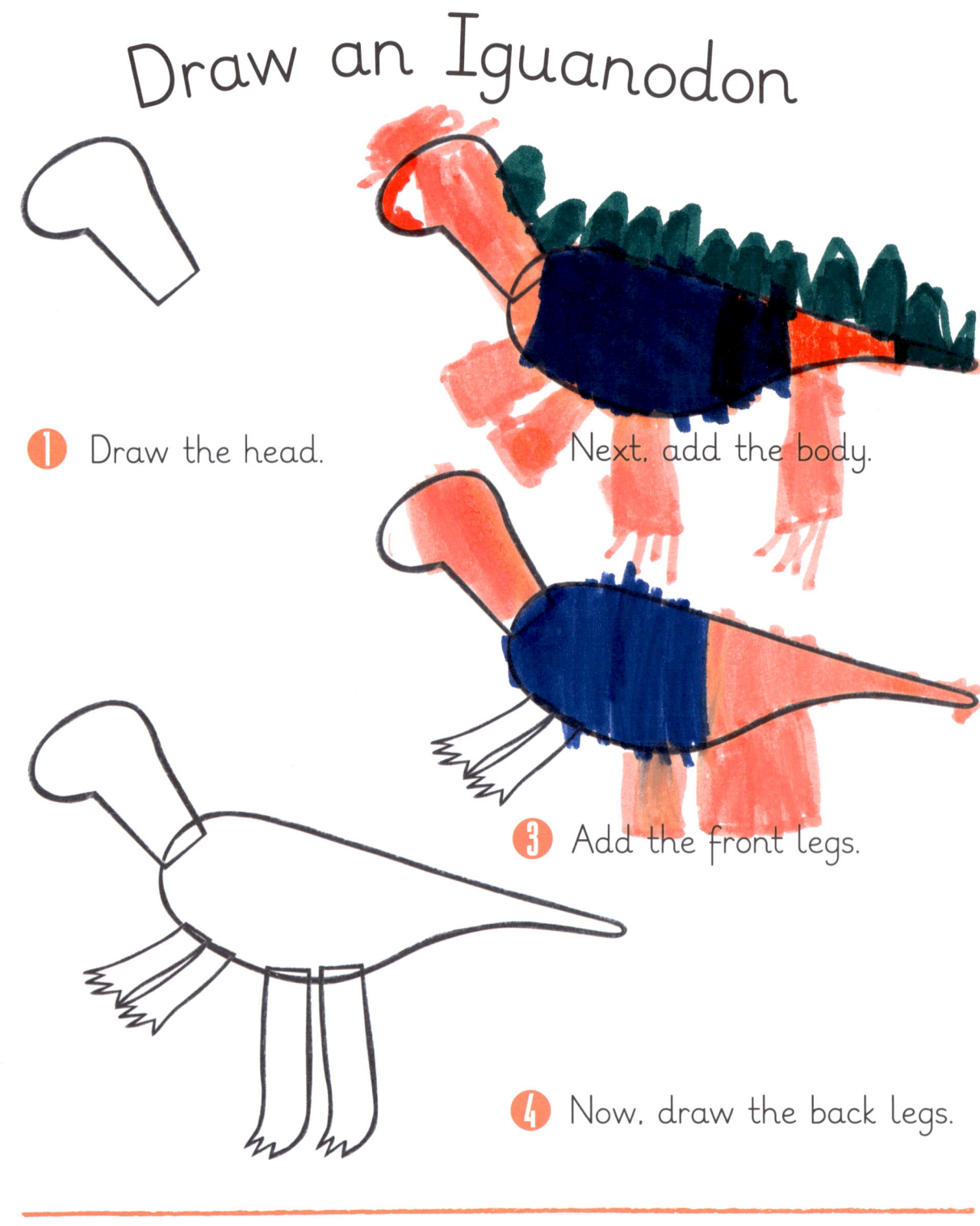

2 Next, add the body.

3 Add the front legs.

4 Now, draw the back legs.

Find the Iguanodon pieces at the back of the book. Set them out in front of you like this:

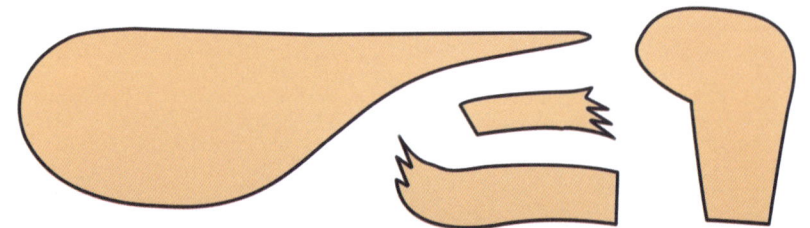

Color your Iguanodon to make it into a funny character! Add instruments to make a band!

The Iguanodon ate vegetables, grew to about 40 feet (12 m), and weighed as much as a van!

Draw spikes along the back.

Draw a jacket, bow tie, and hat!

Make your Iguanodon look different!

Turn the head around.

Change the leg and arm positions.

Add clothes and a hat!

29

Draw a Dimetrodon

1. Draw the head and body.

2. Next, add the tail.

3. Add the sail shape.

4. Now, draw the legs.

Find the Dimetrodon pieces at the back of the book. Set them out in front of you like this:

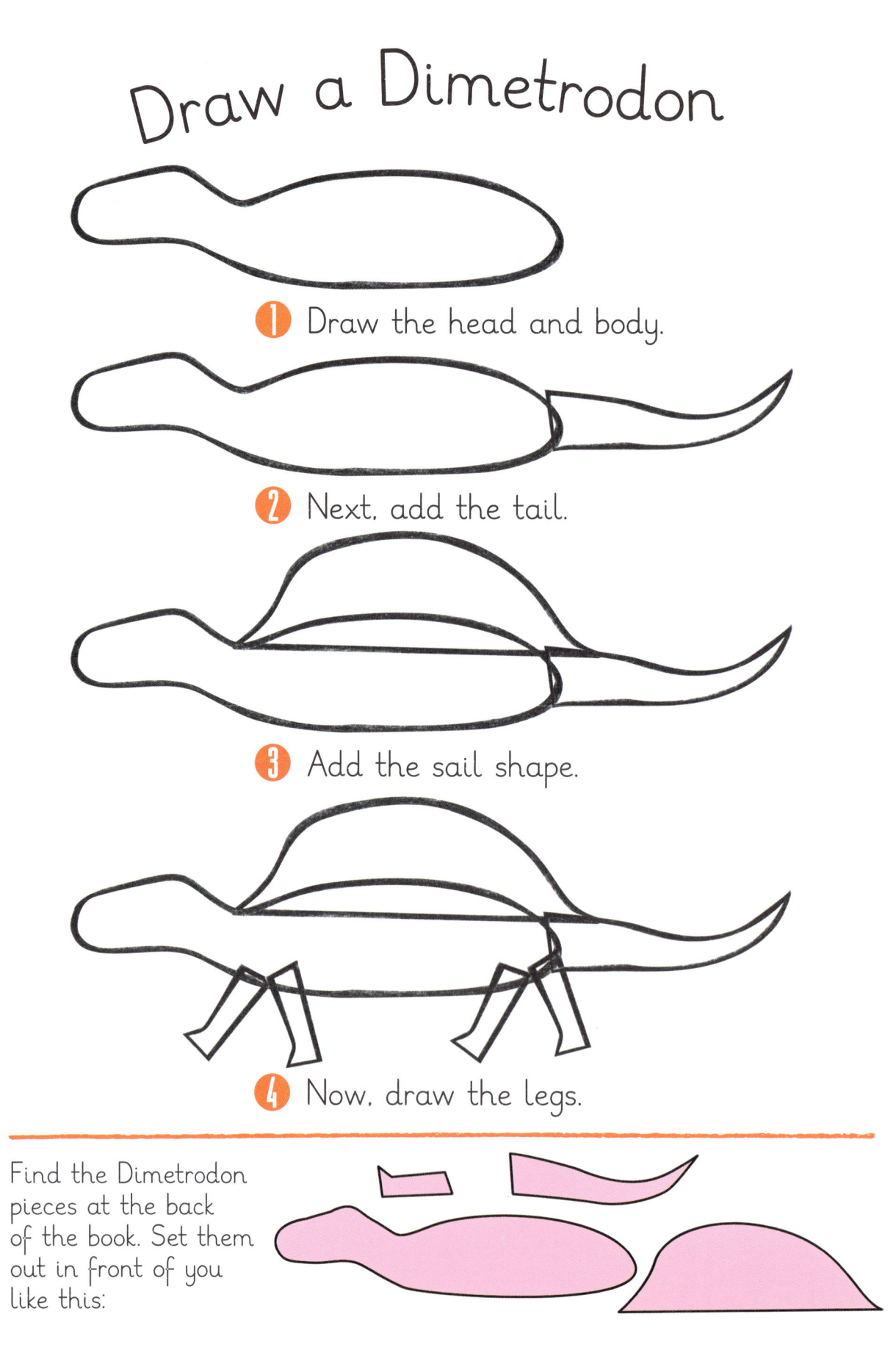

Use your favorite colors.

Color spikes in the sail shape on the back.

The Dimetrodon ate meat and grew to about 15 feet (4.5 m).

Add teeth!

Make your Dimetrodon look different!

This one looks happy!

Make the sail any shape or color you like!

The Dimetrodon is a bit strange—people think of it as a dinosaur, but it existed before the dinosaurs came along!

Draw a Doyouthinkhesaurus

You can invent your own crazy dinosaur by using shapes to draw around from different creatures. Give your animal a funny name. Here's how to draw a Doyouthinkhesaurus!

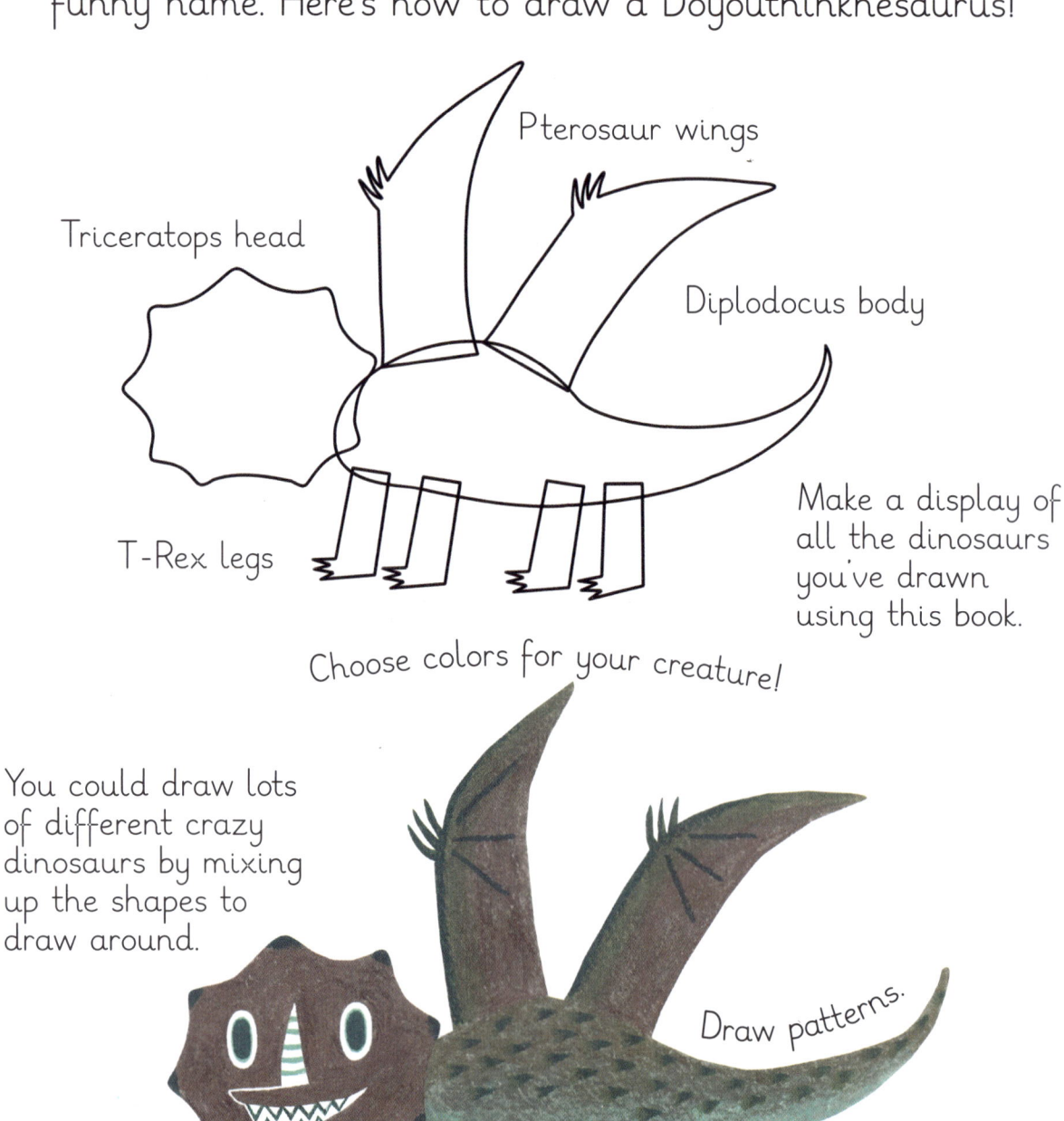

Pterosaur wings

Triceratops head

Diplodocus body

T-Rex legs

Make a display of all the dinosaurs you've drawn using this book.

Choose colors for your creature!

You could draw lots of different crazy dinosaurs by mixing up the shapes to draw around.

Draw patterns.

Have lots of fun!